Caring for My Pet

Dog

Jill Foran

and Katie Gillespie

MEDIA ENHANCED BOOKS

AV2 BY WEIGL

ADDED VALUE • AUDIO VISUAL

www.av2books.com

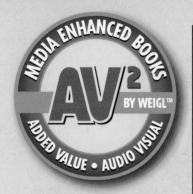

MEDIA ENHANCED BOOKS
AV²
BY WEIGL™
ADDED VALUE • AUDIO VISUAL

AV² provides enriched content that supplements and complements this book. Weigl's AV² books strive to create inspired learning and engage young minds in a total learning experience.

Your AV² Media Enhanced books come alive with...

Audio
Listen to sections of the book read aloud.

Key Words
Study vocabulary, and complete a matching word activity.

Video
Watch informative video clips.

Quizzes
Test your knowledge.

Go to **www.av2books.com**, and enter this book's unique code.

BOOK CODE

W 6 8 0 3 6 0

Embedded Weblinks
Gain additional information for research.

Slide Show
View images and captions, and prepare a presentation.

AV² by Weigl brings you media enhanced books that support active learning.

Try This!
Complete activities and hands-on experiments.

... and much, much more!

Published by AV² by Weigl
350 5th Avenue, 59th Floor
New York, NY 10118
Website: www.av2books.com www.weigl.com

Library of Congress Control Number: 2013953117
ISBN 978-1-4896-0608-2 (hardcover)
ISBN 978-1-4896-0609-9 (softcover)
ISBN 978-1-4896-0610-5 (single user eBook)
ISBN 978-1-4896-0611-2 (multi-user eBook)

Printed in the United States of America in North Mankato, Minnesota
1 2 3 4 5 6 7 8 9 0 18 17 16 15 14

012014
WEP301113

Project Coordinator: Katie Gillespie
Design and Layout: Mandy Christiansen

Weigl acknowledges Getty Images as its primary image supplier for this title. Page 22: Mark Wilson

Dog

Contents

Puppy Pals

People all over the world keep dogs as pets. Dogs are intelligent, faithful, and extremely loving animals. A dog can comfort you when you are feeling sad or lonely. She can also be trained to perform important jobs. There are special guide dogs, police dogs, and herding dogs. For many reasons, adding a canine companion to your family can be a rewarding experience.

However, despite their positive qualities, it is not easy to own a dog. They require a lot of time and commitment. Dogs must be fed, groomed, played with, and cared for on a daily basis. If you are willing to be patient, the love that you receive from your dog will make the effort of caring for her worthwhile.

1/3 of all **American households** own a dog.

There is only **one species** of domestic dog.

For **thousands of years**, dogs have been loyal human companions.

10% of dog **owners** in the U.S. have **three or more dogs**.

Physical activity is important for maintaining your dog's health. Most dogs should be taken outdoors twice a day to exercise.

From Wild to Mild

Dogs have lived on Earth for many years. The majority of scientists agree that all species of dogs, including wolves, foxes, coyotes, and domestic dogs, **evolved** from the same creature. This animal was a weasel-like, tree-climbing mammal known as *Miacis*.

Wolves and dogs are closely related. They share several characteristics, such as strength, speed, and a tendency to travel in packs.

Out of all the animals in the world, dogs have been associated with people the longest. It is believed that thousands of years ago, dogs visited human villages to look for discarded food. In exchange for guarding livestock, assisting with hunting, and warning of danger, people offered dogs food and shelter.

Soon, humans discovered how useful dogs could be. They grew to depend on dogs, both for protection and for companionship. Over time, dogs began to be bred to meet specific needs.

Miacis dates back **50 million** years.

There were at least **five types of dog** in existence in **4,500 BC**.

Dogs were the **first domesticated animals.**

Playing fetch with your dog is a great form of exercise. Some dogs can even be trained to bring objects such as the daily newspaper or mail.

Pet Profile

There are several different dog breeds to choose from. You must learn more about the ones that interest you before buying a new pet. Dog breeds are grouped according to their roles, behavior, and features. Each breed has certain characteristics that make it unique. Think about the dog features that are most important to you and your family.

Golden Retrievers

- Belong to the **sporting group**
- Are one of the world's most popular household dogs
- Have a dense coat that repels water
- Are very friendly and eager to please
- Respected for their tracking abilities
- Are a patient breed

Basenjis

- Belong to the **hound group**
- Are **tricolor**, chestnut red, or black in color
- Have a short, smooth coat
- Are an extremely affectionate breed
- Were once used as hunting dogs in Africa
- Are very patient
- Enjoy being independent

Chinese Shar-peis

- Belong to the **non-sporting group**
- Have a rough **coat** and wrinkled skin
- Are one of the oldest recognized breeds, dating back more than 2,200 years
- Have an average life span of 7 to 10 years
- Prefer the company of humans
- Were once used as fighting dogs in China
- Have a large head

Border Collies

- Belong to the **herding group**
- Are usually black in color
- Have white markings
- Are very energetic and intelligent
- Considered the best sheep-herding dog on Earth
- Are eager to please

Siberian Huskies

- Belong to the **working group**
- Can have brown or blue eyes, or even one of each color
- Are very friendly
- Have a gentle temperament
- Require a lot of exercise
- Are used to pull sleds in certain cold climates

Chihuahuas

- Belong to the **toy group**
- Have a dome-shaped skull
- Are the smallest dog breed
- Have a long, smooth coat
- Do not like cold weather
- Can be aggressive
- Are curious and alert

Picking Your Pet

Getting a dog is a big commitment. There are many things to consider before you add a furry friend to your family. Does anyone in your home have pet allergies? If so, a poodle or a terrier may be a good choice. Since there are so many different breeds, you should research which types of dog are the best fit for you. Think about these important questions before you choose a dog.

How Much Will My Dog Cost?

Having a dog can be very expensive. However, there are different options available to fit a variety of budgets and lifestyles. You can buy your dog from a breeder or a pet store.

This can be costly, but may be worth the price. **Purebred** dogs are typically the most expensive. Alternatively, you may want to rescue your dog from an animal shelter. This will cost much less, and give an animal in need a loving home. You should factor in the cost of food, **veterinary** care, and other supplies your dog will need as well. These costs are ongoing throughout your dog's lifetime.

What Do I Have Time For?

Puppies are cute, but they require a lot more care and attention than an adult dog. It is important to be realistic about the amount of time and energy you have to spend with your dog. Certain breeds may need extra time for training. Long-haired dogs **shed** more than short-haired dogs. They also require additional grooming. Make sure you choose a dog that you will be able to care for properly.

The smallest dog in history was **2.5 inches** tall. (6.4 centimeters)

Dogs have **18** muscles in each ear.

A dog has **three eyelids**.

20%**of owned dogs** in the U.S. were adopted from animal shelters.

2.7 million healthy shelter pets are not adopted each year.

Many dogs turn around three times before they go to sleep. This instinct dates back to wild dogs, who did this to pat the grass down before they slept on it.

Life Cycle

As your pet grows older, he will have different requirements. You should know what your dog needs at each stage in his development. No matter how old your dog is, he must be given lots of love and affection.

Newborn Puppy

Newborn puppies are almost totally helpless when they are born. They cannot walk, and are both deaf and blind. Newborn puppies spend plenty of time drinking their mothers' milk. They also sleep for long periods. It is important for newborn puppies to be kept warm.

Three to Nine Weeks

At three weeks old, puppies are able to see, hear, and walk. By four weeks of age, they are ready to begin exploring. They are ready to be weaned when their teeth start to grow. This occurs sometime between four and seven weeks. At nine weeks, they are ready to eat puppy food. Puppies must stay with their mother and **littermates** until they are at least eight weeks old.

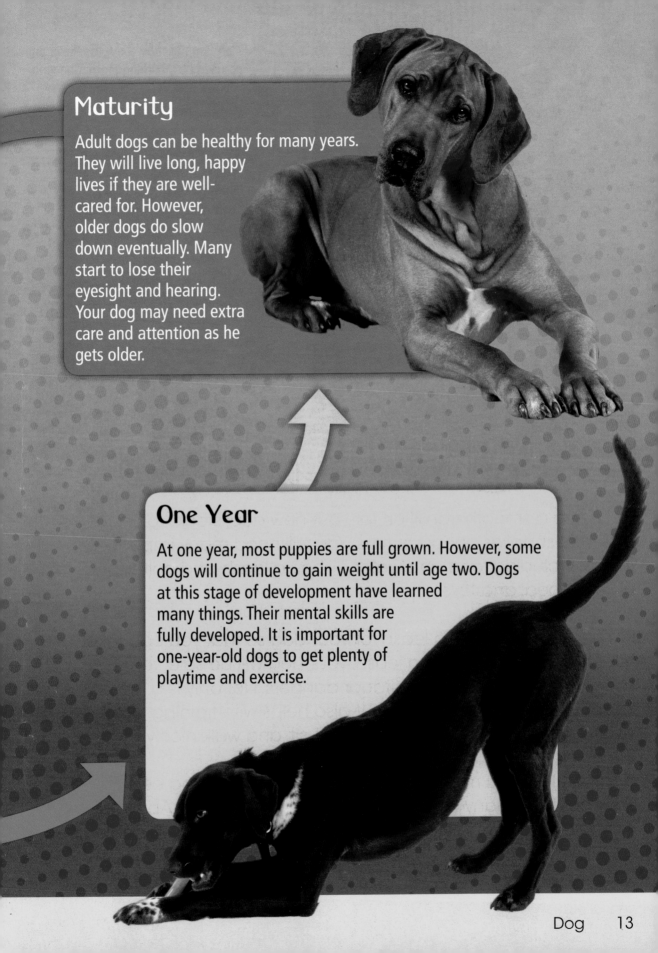

Maturity

Adult dogs can be healthy for many years. They will live long, happy lives if they are well-cared for. However, older dogs do slow down eventually. Many start to lose their eyesight and hearing. Your dog may need extra care and attention as he gets older.

One Year

At one year, most puppies are full grown. However, some dogs will continue to gain weight until age two. Dogs at this stage of development have learned many things. Their mental skills are fully developed. It is important for one-year-old dogs to get plenty of playtime and exercise.

Puppies may chew to relieve pain caused by incoming teeth. Chewing helps older dogs keep their teeth clean and strengthens their jaws.

Dog Supplies

To ensure a smooth transition for your new dog, stock up on the essential supplies ahead of time. You will need many important things, including food and water dishes, a leash and collar, a brush, a bed, and toys.

It is necessary to own a leash for your dog so that you can take her for walks. By wearing a leash, your dog will be safe from speeding cars and other outdoor dangers. Not only is a leash important for your dog's safety, it also helps with training. Use your dog's leash to teach her to heal, sit, and walk nicely.

Another item you must have for your new pet is a dog bed. They come in many different shapes, sizes, and styles. Above all, it should be soft and warm to make your dog feel comfortable.

Place your dog's bed in a quiet area of her own to keep her happy. You can even put a hot-water bottle in her bed if she is nervous. This will remind her of the warmth of her mother and littermates, and help to calm her down.

When choosing toys for your dog, make sure you select ones that are an appropriate strength and size. Dogs, especially puppies, love to chew. Toys that are too weak or too small may be accidentally swallowed. This can be very dangerous for your pet.

Dogs were domesticated more than 10,000 years ago.

A dog's sense of smell is **1 million times better** than a human's.

The basenji is the **only breed** of dog that cannot bark.

There are about 400 million dogs on Earth.

Puppies open their eyes and ears between **10 and 14 days** of age.

Some dogs can identify moving objects from 2,900 feet away. (884 meters)

Taking your dog to the park or walking her on a leash is a fun adventure for both of you. Walks help your dog get used to different sights, sounds, and smells.

Dog Diets

There are many different kinds and brands of dog food. It comes dry, in the form of kibble. Dog food can also be wet and stored in a can. There are even special formulas available for young puppies and senior dogs.

You can buy dog food from a veterinary clinic, pet store, or grocery store. To make sure that you are feeding your dog the right type of food, talk to your **veterinarian**. She will know which brands are best suited to your breed of dog.

It is also important to find out how much you should feed your dog, and how often. Your veterinarian will advise you on the correct amount to feed your dog at all stages of his development.

🐾 Just like people, dogs need the right foods to grow healthy and strong. Make sure to provide your dog with a variety of vegetables and protein.

Young dogs need more frequent meals than older dogs. It is a good idea to feed your dog at the same times every day. Always make sure your dog has a dish full of fresh water to drink.

When your dog is training or exhibiting good behavior, you can feed him treats. Dog biscuits are a good choice because they help keep your dog's teeth healthy. Be careful not to give your dog too many treats. They may lack the nutrients your dog needs. It is essential to feed your dog a balanced diet.

Your dog should be fed from a stainless steel dish. It will be stronger than a plastic dish and will hold up better to dogs that like to chew.

The world's smallest dog weighed only **4 ounces**. (113 grams)

Puppies should eat at least **three meals a day** until they are **three months old**.

Puppies develop their **first full set of baby teeth** by **four weeks** of age.

Adult dogs should be fed **once or twice a day.**

A dog's nose has **four times as many** scent cells as a cat's.

From Nose to Toes

Dogs come in a wide variety of shapes, sizes, and colors. Ranging from the tiny Chihuahua to the gigantic Irish wolfhound, many dog breeds look quite different from one another. However, despite these differences, all dogs share the same **ancestors**. For this reason, all dogs have a number of similar physical features.

Tail

A dog uses her tail to communicate emotions. A tucked in tail indicates fear, while a wagging tail may show that she is happy or excited.

Toes

A dog's feet are long and slender. Dogs always walk and run on their toes.

Paws

Dogs have tough pads on the bottoms of their paws. These pads are used to absorb shock.

Ears

Dogs have a keen sense of hearing. This is because their ears are excellent sound receivers and locators.

Eyes

Dogs have trouble seeing objects that are far away. Their eyesight is not as good as a human's eyesight.

Whiskers

A dog has whiskers on her chin, **muzzle**, and cheeks. She uses them to touch and feel her surroundings.

Teeth

Dogs have very sharp canine teeth that are used to hold **prey**. Their molars are good for grinding food.

Nose

A dog's nose is extremely sensitive. She uses it to smell and identify things, and to control her body temperature.

Great Grooming

Keeping your dog clean is a major responsibility. You must groom your dog's ears, paws, and coat regularly. This will ensure that he is looking and feeling his best. Depending on his breed, your dog will require a particular amount of grooming. Short-haired dogs need less attention than long-haired dogs.

Some dog breeds shed more than others. Brushing your dog will reduce the amount your dog sheds so that extra hair does not build up around your home.

Always brush your dog's fur in the same direction that it grows. Start with his back, then hold his head up to brush down his throat. Next, brush between his front legs. Be very careful when brushing your dog's stomach. The hairs here are fine, and his skin is more sensitive, so it is important to be gentle.

Grooming your dog's coat will help remove dirt. Regular brushing also massages your dog's skin, and promotes circulation. It is important to brush your dog often to help keep him clean.

Most dogs do not need to be bathed very often. If their coats are well-maintained, and they spend the majority of their time indoors, they should only require three or four baths a year. When bathing your dog, use a shampoo designed for dogs or puppies. This will be gentler than a regular shampoo. Also, make sure to restrain your dog so he does not struggle and hurt himself.

Dogs should be taken to the veterinarian for a checkup **once a year.**

A dog's ears should be cleaned **every few weeks.**

The **four areas** that must be **groomed** regularly are the **coat, nails, ears,** and **mouth.**

The world's **first dog show** was held in **1859.**

Best in Show

🐾 You should bathe your pet indoors, unless it is a warm, sunny day. Make sure to place a rubber mat on the bottom of the basin or bathtub to prevent your dog from slipping.

Dogs communicate with people in many ways besides barking. You can tell if your dog is happy by her facial expression and the position of her ears.

Healthy and Happy

In general, dogs are fairly healthy animals. However, there are steps you can take to ensure your dog stays in top condition. Proper grooming and feeding will help keep your dog healthy. Check your dog every day to see if she has split toenails, ticks, or fleas.

Your dog also needs plenty of exercise. Playing with her and taking her for daily walks will help your dog stay in good shape. It is necessary for your dog to maintain a proper weight. Dogs who do not get enough exercise may become overweight. They are also at a higher risk to develop heart disease.

When you first get your dog, you should bring her to a veterinarian. He will examine your dog and let you know if any **vaccinations** should be given. In most countries, the law states that your dog must be vaccinated each year. These shots protect your dog against **rabies** and other dog diseases. Regular checkups are also an important part of maintaining your dog's health.

A puppy should get her **first vaccinations** at **six to eight weeks old.**

83.3 million dogs were owned in the U.S. in **2013.**

Americans spend an average of **$231** on annual veterinary visits.

83% of owned dogs in the U.S. are **spayed** or **neutered**.

There are **3,500 animal shelters** in the United States.

Giving your pet an injection can be dangerous. It is best to have a veterinarian carry out this kind of treatment. Medications in pill or liquid form may be given at home.

Dog Duties

Dogs are incredibly social animals. Years ago, when they lived in the wilderness, dogs were part of groups called packs. Every dog pack had a leader to make the rules. The leader was also responsible for watching over the other group members.

Today, most dogs think of their human family as their pack. It is important to show your dog who is the leader early on. Otherwise, he will become confused. Your dog may even try to take on the role of leader himself. You, or someone in your household, must take charge of the family pack.

Several dog breeds can be trained to enter special competitions, such as agility and obedience contests.

Dogs are extremely intelligent. They can be trained to do many things. It is essential to teach your dog how to behave properly around other animals, especially other dogs. The best way to do this is to familiarize your dog with other animals. Let him meet new dogs so that he becomes comfortable around them. This will also make your dog a better walking companion.

Some common commands you should teach your dog include "sit," "stay," down," "heel," and "come." It is best to start training your dog while he is still a puppy. Puppies are trained more easily than adult dogs. To help train your dog, you can take special classes at an obedience school. There are also many books available on the subject.

Pet Peeves

Dogs do not like:
- being left in a hot car
- people with umbrellas
- having their feet touched
- being home alone all day
- nervous strangers
- people in uniforms
- not having enough water in their bowl

The world record for constant barking is held by a cocker spaniel who barked **907 times** in only **10 minutes**.

Labradors are the **most popular breed** of dog in the world.

Left un-neutered, one pair of dogs and their offspring could produce **67,000** dogs over **six years.**

Always use positive reinforcement when training your dog. Praise him when he does something right, such as sitting on command.

Lassie Come Home and *Courage of Lassie* both feature actress Elizabeth Taylor.

Role Call

Dogs have appeared in countless books, commercials, television shows, and films. The first movie to star a dog was made in England in 1905. It was called *Rescued by Rover*.

One of the most famous dog characters is a collie named Lassie. She first appeared in the book *Lassie Come Home*. Written in 1940, the story is about a dog who is sold to new owners. She has to move from Yorkshire, England all the way to Scotland. Lassie's adventures start when she tries to make the long journey back home. The character has also been featured on television and in films.

Many dogs are trained to carry out important jobs in society. Guard dogs protect private homes and businesses from intruders. Herding dogs help farmers look after livestock. Dogs can even be taught to help people who are in wheelchairs.

Police and fire dogs learn how to protect people and find illegal items, such as explosives. Some breeds, such as Newfoundland dogs, are used as lifeguards on beaches. Rescue dogs can locate drowning victims. They can also sniff out survivors of earthquakes, avalanches, or other disasters.

In **1957**, a dog named Laika became the **first creature to orbit Earth** in a satellite.

Lassie made her television debut in **1954**.

The phrase **"man's best friend,"** originated in **1870**.

Some dog breeds can be trained to help people in need. Rhodesian ridgebacks are often used as companion dogs.

Pet Puzzlers

What do you know about dogs? If you can answer the following questions correctly, you may be ready to own a dog.

1. How many muscles are in a dog's ear?

18

2. Why do dogs wag their tails?

To communicate that they are happy or excited

3. How much did the world's smallest dog weigh?

4 ounces (113 grams)

4. What are the common commands you should teach your pet dog?

"sit," "stay," "down," "heel," and "come"

5. What is the name of the ancient mammal that all dogs evolved from?

Miacis

6. What is a vaccination?

A shot that protects your dog against rabies and other dog diseases

7. How many species of domestic dog are there?

One

8. At what age are a dog's mental skills fully developed?

One year

9. Which breed of dog dates back more than 2,200 years?

Chinese shar-pei

10. What important supplies must you get before bringing a dog home?

Food and water dishes, a leash and collar, a brush, a bed, and toys

Dog Tags

Before you buy your pet dog, brainstorm some dog names you like. Some names may work better for a female dog. Others may suit a male dog. Here are just a few suggestions.

Charlie

Rover

Max

Benji

Spot

Lucy

Molly

Sam

Jake

Key Words

ancestors: early animals from which later species developed

coat: a dog's fur

evolved: developed gradually over time

herding group: breeds used to control the movement of other animals

hound group: breeds that search for hunted animals by smell and sight

littermates: a group of animals born at the same time

muzzle: the part of an animal's face that juts out and includes the jaw, mouth, and nose

non-sporting group: breeds of sturdy dogs that include a variety of types

prey: animals that are hunted and killed by other animals for food

purebred: an animal whose relatives are known and in whom the same traits have been passed down through generations

rabies: a disease that can cause death

shed: lose fur

sporting group: breeds noted for being active and alert; good in the water

toy group: breeds noted for their small size

tricolor: having three colors

vaccinations: injections of medicines that help prevent certain diseases

veterinarian: animal doctor

veterinary: medical treatment of animals

working group: breeds noted for their large size and strength

Index

Log on to www.av2books.com

AV² by Weigl brings you media enhanced books that support active learning. Go to www.av2books.com, and enter the special code found on page 2 of this book. You will gain access to enriched and enhanced content that supplements and complements this book. Content includes video, audio, weblinks, quizzes, a slide show, and activities.

AV² Online Navigation

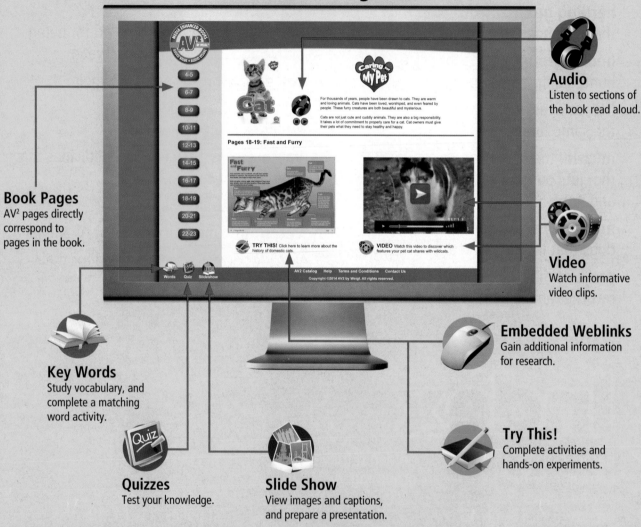

Audio
Listen to sections of the book read aloud.

Book Pages
AV² pages directly correspond to pages in the book.

Video
Watch informative video clips.

Key Words
Study vocabulary, and complete a matching word activity.

Embedded Weblinks
Gain additional information for research.

Try This!
Complete activities and hands-on experiments.

Quizzes
Test your knowledge.

Slide Show
View images and captions, and prepare a presentation.

AV² was built to bridge the gap between print and digital. We encourage you to tell us what you like and what you want to see in the future.

Sign up to be an AV² Ambassador at www.av2books.com/ambassador.

Due to the dynamic nature of the Internet, some of the URLs and activities provided as part of AV² by Weigl may have changed or ceased to exist. AV² by Weigl accepts no responsibility for any such changes. All media enhanced books are regularly monitored to update addresses and sites in a timely manner. Contact AV² by Weigl at 1-866-649-3445 or av2books@weigl.com with any questions, comments, or feedback.